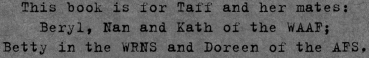

This book is for Taff and her mates:
Beryl, Nan and Kath of the WAAF;
Betty in the WRNS and Doreen of the AFS.

Thanks to:

Bletchley Park Museum's Victoria Worpole,
Director of Education, and Stephen Ovens,
Archivist. Also Wendy Weddell, who kindly
allowed us access to the memorabilia of her
mum, WAAF Section Officer Paddy Fraser.

JANETTA OTTER-BARRY BOOKS

Taff in the WAAF © Frances Lincoln Limited 2010
Text and illustrations © Mick Manning and Brita Granström 2010

First published in Great Britain in 2010 and in the USA in 2011 by
Frances Lincoln Children's Books,
4 Torriano Mews, Torriano Avenue
London NW5 2RZ
www.franceslincoln.com

All rights reserved

No part of this publication may be reproduced, stored in a retrieval system,
or transmitted, in any form, or by any means, electrical, mechanical,
photocopying, recording or otherwise without the prior written
permission of the publisher or a licence permitting restricted copying.
In the United Kingdom such licences are issued by the
Copyright Licensing Agency, Saffron House,
6-10 Kirby Street, London EC1N 8TS

A catalogue record for this book is available from the British Library

ISBN 978-1-84780-093-0

Illustrated in pencil and watercolour

Set in Trixie

Printed in Dongguan, Guangdong, China
by Toppan Leefung in June 2010

1 2 3 4 5 6 7 8 9

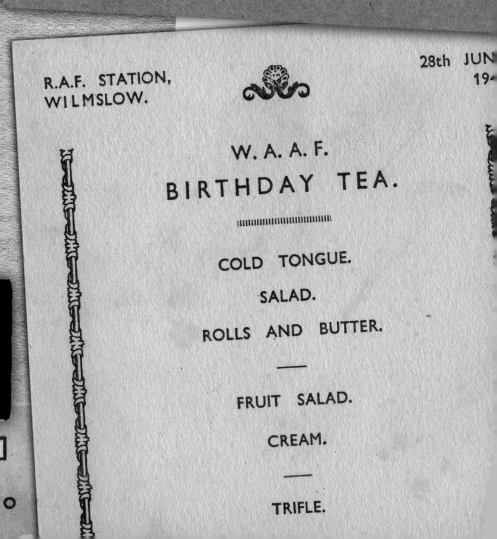

R.A.F. STATION,
WILMSLOW.

28th JUN
19

W. A. A. F.
BIRTHDAY TEA.

COLD TONGUE.

SALAD.

ROLLS AND BUTTER.

—

FRUIT SALAD.

CREAM.

—

TRIFLE.

WITH THE W.A.A.F.

Taff in the WAAF

MICK MANNING & BRITA GRANSTRÖM

During World War Two my mum was a wireless operator in the top secret 'Y' service. Here's her story – a story she kept quiet for years.

Mick

F

FRANCES LINCOLN
CHILDREN'S BOOKS

MY SISTERS AND I COULDN'T SWIM,
BUT WE'D PRETEND BY HOPPING ON ONE LEG!
WHAT A LAUGH!

MUM'S RABBIT PIE WAS SO TASTY I FORGOT
TO FEEL SORRY FOR THE BUNNY - BUT I
STILL REMEMBER THE SONG:

RUN RABBIT - RUN RABBIT! RUN! RUN! RUN!

THIS SPACE FOR COMMUNICATION

POST CARD

P.C. 2.30 AM

WYN BAY

COLWYN BAY

I grew up in a seaside town in Wales
where every day felt like a holiday.
But my world changed for ever when
Adolf Hitler invaded Poland in 1939.
There was no TV back then and by 1940
the radio had become our window on to
a world at war. We listened in horror
as Europe fell to the German army,
and worried Britain would be next.

WAR SAVINGS
are War Weapons

WAR

Young men were called up to fight — they had no choice. Lorries full of new recruits sped through our town. At night our dog barked at trains thundering past our house. Loaded with war supplies, they fumed smoke and sparks like angry Welsh dragons!

MANY CONVOY SHIPS CARRYING FOOD SUPPLIES FROM THE USA WERE TORPEDOED AND SUNK BY THE NAZI U-BOATS.

YOU NAZI SPY!

RUMOURS WENT ROUND. ONE NIGHT I SAW A MAN LURKING IN THE SHADOWS... MUM RAN OUT WITH A POKER BUT HE WAS JUST A LODGER STAYING NEXT DOOR!

EARLY IN THE WAR, BECAUSE OF THE FEAR OF POISON GAS, EVERYONE CARRIED A GAS MASK - JUST IN CASE.

I WOULDN'T DARE!

I'M GOING TO ASK FOR EXTRA!

RATIONING

By 1940 I was working in a grocer's with my friend Beryl. We had to limit the quantity of food people could buy according to the ration coupons they had, and that meant queues. Once, a woman tried to get me to give her extra bacon. When I refused, the cheeky goose accused me of giving her short rations! I had to go to court – but I proved her wrong!

BRITISH CITIES, SHIPYARDS AND FACTORIES WERE HEAVILY BOMBED BY THE LUFTWAFFE IN 1940 — IT BECAME KNOWN AS 'THE BLITZ'.

AIR RAID PRECAUTIONS

HANDBOOK No. 2
Amended Reprint
June, 1940

THE BLITZ

One weekend, visiting my cousins in Tyneside, I heard an eerie wailing noise. Air raid sirens! Searchlights lit up the sky. Enemy bombers droned overhead! We ran to the Anderson shelter in the garden. It smelled of tomcats; but as the bombs began exploding across the shipyards and the earth shook with every blast, it felt like the safest place in the world.

WOMEN VOLUNTEERS SOMETIMES OPERATED ANTI-AIRCRAFT GUNS ...

DOREEN, ONE OF MY FRIENDS, WAS A VOLUNTEER IN THE AUXILIARY FIRE SERVICE - A VERY DANGEROUS JOB.

KEEP CALM AND CARRY ON

CALLING V FOR VICTOR; COME IN V FOR VICTOR...

THE WOMEN'S AUXILIARY AIR FORCE WAS THE WOMEN'S BRANCH OF THE RAF.

...V FOR VICTOR HERE: TALLY HO!

THE RAF ARE WINNING THE BATTLE OF BRITAIN...

HELP THE R.A.F
JOIN THE WAAF

G R
MINISTRY OF LABOUR
THE MINISTRY OF FOOD
GIRLS
Aged 16-18 Years
The Food Question is A Woman's Question
Come and Help the Food M
They want you NO

APPLY WAAF RECRUTING OFFICE

MINISTRY OF FOOD

I arrived home in Wales to find Beryl had joined the WAAF! It didn't feel the same in the shop without her, so when the Ministry of Food was evacuated to our little town I got a job there. Writing down the amounts of powdered milk delivered by the Atlantic convoys was pretty boring. I was helping the war effort, but somehow I felt I should do more.

MINISTRY OF FOOD
WAR COOKERY LEAFLET 11

Number

BERYL TOLD ME SHE WAS AN ARMOURER, LOADING BOMBS ON AN RAF AIRFIELD.

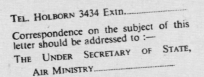

JOINING THE WAAF

I don't know what made me join the WAAF!
But I did! Soon a letter arrived from the
Air Ministry ordering me to report to a WAAF
training centre. I was kitted out with a
uniform and I got a nickname too — 'Taff'
because I was Welsh. So here was 'Taff'
joining the WAAF, joining the war.

YOU'LL BE POSTED TO CHICKSANDS 'Y' STATION.

TOP SECRET!
NAZI HQ
ENEMY SENDS MESSAGE
OUR 'Y' STATIONS INTERCEPT THE MESSAGE WITHOUT NAZIS KNOWING!
WE LEARN THEIR SECRET PLANS!
THE 'Y' SERVICE CAN SHORTEN THE WAR!!

BERYL WROTE THAT SHE'D BECOME A 'FLYING NIGHTINGALE', A WAAF NURSE.

LESSON 5.

Dah	Dit	N	—·
Dah	D'	Dit	D	—··
Dah	D'	D'	Dit	B	—···

MORSE CODE

I trained to be a wireless operator. The 'dah-dit-dah' of Morse code echoing in my headset made my ears ring! When I'd learnt to 'send' and 'receive' I got my 'Sparks' badge. A man from MI5 came to talk to us. We signed the official secrets act before he told us about the 'Y' service. 'Listening in' to enemy messages, he promised, would shorten the war — so I volunteered.

WAAFS DID ALL SORTS OF JOBS: FROM PLOTTERS TO COOKS, CLERKS AND MECHANICS.

SOME WAAFS, INCLUDING NOOR INAYAT KHAN, BECAME SOE AGENTS. HOW CAN WE FORGET THEIR HEROISM?

WE'LL MEET AGAIN. DON'T KNOW WHERE, DON'T KNOW WHEN ...

IS IT BAD NEWS?

WE'D TAKE TURNS CHOOSING A SONG TO SING. IT CHEERED US UP BETTER THAN A CUP OF NAAFI COCOA!

SHALL WE GO DANCING ON FRIDAY?

WAAF slang:
Dim as a NAAFI candle — Stupid!
Blackouts — Winter knickers
Twilights — Summer knickers
Queen Bee — WAAF officer
Sparks — Wireless operators
TTFN — Ta-ta for now
Hush-hush — Top secret

CHICKSANDS

Form 295.
(In pads of 100.)

Chicksands 'Y' station was in the grounds of a haunted priory. I never met the ghost but I met lots of other WAAFs: tall ones, short ones, bossy ones and shy ones. We were all homesick together - laughing and crying, talking about our families and our friends caught up in that terrible war.

SEND A MESSAGE TO HEADQUARTERS.

JA, KAPITÄN!

THE 'Y' SERVICE

We worked in shifts, day and night, turning a dial to search the airwaves for Nazi 'Traffic'. Suddenly, out of the crackly background noise, enemy Morse code would hit my eardrums at 90 letters a minute. Getting the whole message down without any mistakes was my way of fighting back. I'd imagine who was 'sending' and shudder.

Form 96.

MESSAGE FORM
(Above this line is for Signals use only)
Signal Office File No.

THE GERMANS USED A SPECIAL DEVICE CALLED ENIGMA TO KEEP THEIR MESSAGES SECRET. THE TO AND FRO OF MESSAGES ON THE AIRWAVES WAS CALLED 'TRAFFIC'.

ON AVERAGE 3,000 INTERCEPTS A DAY CAME TO BLETCHLEY, SOME BY BIKE AND SOME BY TELEPRINTER.

MANY BIKE MESSENGERS WERE GIRLS FROM THE ATS, SOME OF WHOM DROVE MOTORBIKES AND LORRIES.

STNX   6

CKS 11 29/11/44 1656 5147A C2016/7/ A295

BLETCHLEY PARK

Our 'intercepts' - the blocks of code we wrote down - made no sense to us, but we guessed that someone somewhere must be decoding them. We didn't know back then, but the intercepts were rushed to a place called Bletchley Park. Here, mathematicians were using brainpower to fight back and crack the Germans' codes.

THIS ONE'S TOP PRIORITY!

TOP SECRET

ENIGMA MACHINES LOOKED A BIT LIKE TYPEWRITERS BUT COULD ENCRYPT MESSAGES IN 150 MILLION, MILLION, MILLION DIFFERENT WAYS!

CODE-BREAKERS LOOKED FOR COMMON PHRASES. THIS 'CRIB' WAS THEN GIVEN TO A BOMBE WHICH ELECTRO-MECHANICALLY CALCULATED COMBINATIONS OF LETTERS. THIS COULD TAKE HOURS - OR DAYS.

ALAN TURING WAS A LEADING MATHEMATICIAN AT BLETCHLEY. HE DEVISED MANY SUCCESSFUL TECHNIQUES FOR CRACKING ENIGMA CODES, INCLUDING THE BOMBE.

ANY LUCK?

NO, THIS ONE'S TAKING DAYS TO CRACK.

THE BOMBE

Because they changed their code settings every day, the Nazis believed Enigma was unbreakable. But they didn't know that secret Polish research into Enigma had been sent to help Bletchley design huge, noisy, robot-calculators called Bombes. These electric machines never slept and worked day and night. Slowly Bletchley began to read the Nazis' secrets.

COLOSSUS WAS BUILT IN 1943 TO CRACK ANOTHER NAZI CODE MACHINE CALLED LORENZ. IT WAS THE FIRST TRUE COMPUTER.

DOODLEBUG

Form 295.
(In pads of 100.)
R.A.F.CE
421

One day danger came from the sky. We heard the droning sound long before we saw it: a German doodlebug, buzzing along like some monstrous wasp! As it fell to earth we ran for our lives ... Luckily the missile came down in the river or we would have all been blown to pieces.

JOHN HAS A LONG MOUSTACHE ...

CHICKSANDS ALSO SENT CODED MESSAGES HIDDEN IN BBC BROADCASTS: THIS FAMOUS ONE WARNED THE FRENCH RESISTANCE TO PREPARE FOR D-DAY.

WE WORKED IN A BLOCK BEHIND THE NISSEN HUTS SURROUNDED BY TALL RADIO MASTS.

JITTERBUG

By 1944, England was full of allied troops preparing for D-Day. Glenn Miller and his band often played nearby and coachloads of off-duty WAAFs would go to dance with the Yanks. We didn't know it then, but so many of our dancing partners, those jitterbugging young men, would be killed during the D-Day landings ...

EVEN AS THEIR U-BOATS WERE BEING SUNK THE NAZIS STILL BELIEVED THEIR CODES WERE SAFE.

WINSTON CHURCHILL OFTEN VISITED BLETCHLEY PARK. BY D-DAY THE ALLIES KNEW GERMAN TROOP LOCATIONS AND STRENGTHS, SAVING MANY LIVES.

I WAS CHOSEN TO MARCH IN THE FIRST BATTLE OF BRITAIN SERVICE TO REMEMBER THOSE WHO'D DIED.

ME? OH, I'M JUST TAFF IN THE WAAF.

SOMEONE OUGHT TO WRITE A BOOK ABOUT US, TAFF!

WHAT DID TAFF DO IN THE WAR?

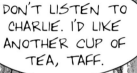

28th JUNE
MENU

PEACE

R.A.F. STATION,
WILMSLOW.

The Germans were finally defeated
in 1945, and I was posted to RAF
Wilmslow. I was put to work in the
sergeants' mess. I went from picking up
Nazi codes to picking up dirty plates.
But I still kept my 'Y' service secret.
When people asked me what I'd done in
the war I'd shrug my shoulders and say
with the sweetest smile, "Me? Oh I was
just a Taff in the WAAF."

The Nazis did terrible things I can't bear to think about. But in the end they were beaten- and not just by bullets, but by brainpower and teamwork. Men and women played their part and we mustn't forget any of them.

Taff

Form 295.
(In pads of 100.)
R.A.F. CENSOR
421

GLOSSARY

AFS - AUXILIARY FIRE SERVICE. Many women joined the Fire Service and tackled blazing buildings during the Blitz.

ATA - AIR TRANSPORT AUXILIARY. It included 166 women pilots who delivered new planes from factory to airfield.

ATS - AUXILIARY TERRITORIAL SERVICE. The women's branch of the army. By 1943 there were 200,000 women in the ATS. Just like the WAAF and the WRNS, jobs varied from cooks and clerks to lorry drivers and motorbike messengers.

AIR RAID SIREN - loud siren warning of an impending bombing raid.

ALAN TURING - one of the key mathematicians at Bletchley Park and the 'father' of all the computers we use today.

ANDERSON SHELTER - a back garden air-raid shelter made of corrugated iron.

BLETCHLEY PARK - also known as Station X, provided crucial information to the allies by decrypting Enigma and Lorenz Codes. This shortened the war, saving many lives. Bletchley Park is now a museum run by the Bletchley Park Trust. It is open to school parties and the public and has a splendid website. Http://www.bletchleypark.org.uk/

BLITZ — short for the German word 'Blitzkrieg', which means 'lightning war'.

BOFFINS — a nickname for inventors, scientists and mathematicians. Many were recruited to work at Bletchley because they could solve a difficult newspaper crossword in under 12 minutes!

BOMBE — the name of a huge electronic calculating machine. Inspired by an earlier Polish design, it was devised by Alan Turing and Gordon Welchman.

CODE — a message which is converted into numbers, letters and symbols to make it secret.

COLOSSUS — the world's first programmable, digital, electronic computer. It was designed by Tommy Flowers and other scientists to solve codes at Bletchley Park and was operating by 1944.

CRYPTOGRAPHER — someone who decodes cryptograms, another word for coded messages.

CHICKSANDS — the major 'Y' Station collecting and supplying Bletchley with intercepted Nazi messages known as 'Traffic'. It also communicated with Resistance groups in Europe by hiding messages in BBC wireless broadcasts.

CONCENTRATION CAMPS — prison camps where millions of Jews, Gypsies and political prisoners were murdered by the Nazis.

COMPUTER — an electronic machine that can be programmed to perform tasks and solve problems.

D-DAY — in June 1944 Britain, America and their allies invaded France and fought their way across Europe. They beat the Germans in 1945.

DECRYPT — to decode an encrypted message to plain words.

DOODLEBUG — the V1 missile was an unpiloted rocket-bomb launched from Nazi bases in Europe. When the fuel ran out it fell to earth and exploded.

ENSA — ENTERTAINMENTS NATIONAL SERVICE ASSOCIATION. Performers like Vera Lynn would entertain workers in factories and troops on the front line, even while the bombs were falling.

ENCRYPT — to convert a message into code.

ENIGMA — a German electro-mechanical rotor machine, invented by Arthur Scherbius, used for encrypting messages.

EVACUEES — many children from heavily bombed cities were evacuated to live in rural areas, often with complete strangers.

HITLER - the leader of the Nazis, who died in 1945, just before Germany was defeated.

LORENZ MACHINE - German cipher machine used during World War II for encrypting 'high-level' German teleprinter messages.

MORSE CODE - a worldwide system, representing numbers and letters of the alphabet by using long or short signals of sound or light.

MUSLIM - a follower of the Islamic religion.

NAAFI - NAVY ARMY AND AIR FORCE INSTITUTION. They served hot drinks and snacks to the troops.

NAZIS - a German political party led by Adolf Hitler. They came to power in 1933 by encouraging patriotism and racism. Believing they were the master-race they arrested and murdered Jewish people, Gypsies and anyone who disagreed with them. Millions of men, women and children were put to death in concentration camps such as Auschwitz and Dachau. Some Germans opposed the Nazis but many kept silent through fear of Hitler and his terrible secret police 'the Gestapo'.

OFFICIAL SECRETS ACT - British laws of secrecy to protect information that might endanger national security.

OZ - stands for ounces, a weight measurement: eg. 4 oz = 113g.

PACIFIST - someone who believes all violence is wrong.

PLOTTERS - charted battle progress by plotting positions on large maps in operation control rooms.

RATION COUPONS - food and clothing had to be rationed during the hard times of the war, and for some years afterwards, to make sure everyone got a fair share.

RUN RABBIT RUN - a popular 1930s song. The lyrics were changed to poke fun at the Nazis:'Run Adolf, Run Adolf, run, run, run'.

SOE - SPECIAL OPERATIONS EXECUTIVE. A British secret service organisation that trained both men and women to work behind enemy lines. Many female SOE agents were executed by the Nazis including: Violette Szabo, Denise Bloch, Elaine Plewman and WAAF officers Yolande Beekman, Diana Rowden, Lilian Rolfe, Cécile Lefort and Noor Inayat Khan.

W.A.A.F. JACKET
292/C/921 N.
Size 3

7 APR 14[?]

H.Q. 10 GROUP, R.A.F.

NOOR INAYAT KHAN – a pre-war children's author and great granddaughter of the Tipoo Sultan of Mysore. Khan was a Muslim who joined the WAAF and SOE despite strong pacifist beliefs. She was captured on active service in France and executed by the Nazis at Dachau concentration camp in 1944.

U-BOAT – the name for a German submarine. Sending messages encrypted by Enigma, the U-boats hunted in packs, sinking thousands of allied ships.

WAAF – WOMENS AUXILIARY AIR FORCE. There were 183,000 WAAFs by 1943 doing dozens of jobs including mechanics, wireless and radar operators, bomb loaders, barrage balloon crews, plotters and SOE agents.

WINSTON CHURCHILL – became the British Prime Minister soon after the Second World War began and proved a strong leader in those dark days.

WIRELESS OPERATORS – also known as Wireless Ops or 'Sparks', were trained to send, listen to and write down radio signals, often using Morse code.

WLA – WOMEN'S LAND ARMY. Volunteers who did back-breaking farm work previously only done by men.

WRNS – WOMEN'S ROYAL NAVAL SERVICE. There were 74,000 'Wrens' by the end of the war: from operations room staff to welders, carpenters, torpedo loaders and motor-boat crews.

WVS – THE WOMEN'S VOLUNTARY SERVICE worked tirelessly to help the war effort at home, running mobile canteens, organising evacuees and helping bombed out families during the Blitz.

WORLD WAR TWO – began in 1939 when Nazi Germany invaded Poland and then many other countries including: Norway, Denmark, Holland, France, Belgium and Greece. The Germans' allies included Japan, Italy, Hungary and Slovakia although Italy later changed sides. The Nazis and their allies were defeated in 1945.

Y STATIONS – a chain of top-secret listening stations that intercepted coded enemy signals and passed them on to Bletchley Park.

Unit To	Reason
Chester.	
Res.	
Wilmslow.	
13 RS.	Ho
3 RS.	Ho
Stn Cheadle (a)	HH
Chicksands	
Cheadle	
Chicksands	X
Wilmslow	X

4 2c

IDENTITY CARD FOR R.A.F. AND
W.A.A.F. PERSONNEL (All Ranks)

This is to certify that No. 2100133
ACW2 JONES E.M.
(Rank and full name)
whose description is contained herein is serving in
the Royal Air Force and is stationed
Women's Auxiliary Air Force
at ....

Changes of rank to be certified below

Date	Rank	Station	Signature and rank of officer certifying
26/8/44	ACW2	3 RS	
15/11/44	ACW2	Stn Cheadle	
18/11/44	ACW2	chicksands	
7/9/45	ACW2	Wilmslow	

Description
Height .... 5'3"   Build .... SMALL.
Colour of eyes .... BLUE   Colour of hair .... FAIR.
Date of birth 28.7.1923

No. 1131046

Signature of holder
E M Jones